IDEAS Plus

A Collection of Practical Teaching Ideas

Book Fifteen

National Council of Teachers of English
1111 W. Kenyon Road, Urbana, Illinois 61801-1096

Project Coordinator: Felice Kaufmann

Staff Editor: Jeannette Kent

Cover Design: Joellen Bryant

Cover/interior photographs: Thompson McClellan Photo

Interior Book Design: Tom Kovacs for TGK Design

NCTE Stock Number: 22787

It is the policy of NCTE in its journals and other publications to provide a forum for the open discussion of ideas concerning the content and the teaching of English and the language arts. Publicity accorded to any particular point of view does not imply endorsement by the Executive Committee, the Board of Directors, or the membership at large, except in announcements of policy, where such endorsement is clearly specified.

Library of Congress Catalog Card Number 84-3479

IDEAS Plus is published in August by the National Council of Teachers of English as an exclusive benefit of *NCTE Plus* membership. *NCTE Plus* membership also includes four issues of *NOTES Plus* (ISSN 0738-86-24), published in October, December, January, and March. Annual membership dues are $55.00; $15.00 of this amount is for *NOTES Plus* and *IDEAS Plus*. Inquiries about *NCTE Plus* membership or communications regarding change of address and permission to reprint should be addressed to *NOTES Plus*, 1111 W. Kenyon Road, Urbana, IL 61801-1096. *POSTMASTER:* Send address changes to *NOTES Plus*, 1111 W. Kenyon Road, Urbana, IL 61801-1096. Periodical postage paid at Urbana, Illinois, and at additional mailing offices.

Contents

Foreword

IDEAS Plus and its quarterly companion *NOTES Plus* are the principal benefits of *NCTE Plus* membership. *IDEAS Plus* is sent out at the end of the summer so that teachers will have it in hand as they begin the school year.

The ideas collected in this fifteenth edition of *IDEAS Plus* come from two sources: ideas submitted at an Idea Exchange session at an NCTE Annual Convention or Spring Conference, and contributions by readers of *NOTES Plus* and *IDEAS Plus*.

1 Prewriting and Writing

Prewriting and writing activities not only help prepare students for the high level of communication skills demanded in the outside world, but they serve other functions as well, such as enhancing self-exploration and self-expression, honing critical thinking, and giving students a sense of control over their environment. The writing exercises and activities presented in this section will help fulfill these goals and also provide a foundation for the many types of writing that students will need later in life.

Enlisting "Readers" for Written Feedback

I ask my students to give a copy of the following reader-response form to at least one adult and one peer as they gather materials for their writing portfolios. I have found that these responses help the families and friends of my students understand both the importance of writing and the value of the writer. The readers' comments provide new perspectives and help students to better evaluate their writing. This idea isn't necessarily tied to portfolios—it could be an effective feedback mechanism for a variety of writing assignments.

Dear _____ ,

Thank you for agreeing to be one of my readers for my English Portfolio this quarter. Your opinion matters to me.

Please read the following piece of writing that I have worked on this quarter. It is entitled _____. It is about _____.

After you have read it, please give me some written feedback about this piece. There is room for your response at the bottom of this sheet. You might tell me what you like best about it, what you wish I had written more about, and/or what you wish I had done differently.

Thank you again for taking the time to read my work and write about your responses to it.

Sincerely,

_____

Response
Title _____

_____
_____
_____
_____
_____

Signed,

_____
_____ (date)

Susan Stevens, Youngstown City Schools, Youngstown, Ohio

Writing Poems for Children

When my son was in second grade he had a very special teacher, Mrs. Petras, who helped him learn to love poetry. She constantly read poems to and with her students. Eventually, my son and a group of friends began writing poetry—at first collaboratively, and finally, on their own. I was so impressed by the ease with which he approached poetry that I developed a poetry project specifically to help students become more comfortable and open to writing poetry.

This project also helps students learn how to: 1) adapt existing material in a new format, 2) write for a specific audience (other than the teacher or peers), 3) work in a group, and finally, 4) unleash their creativity. The end product is a children's book targeted at second and third graders.

I begin the project by bringing in many children's books. Over the years, I have tried to find newer books that my students would not have read as children; every year, however, at least one group will ask if they may do an old favorite (for example, *Strega Nona* or *The True Story of the Three Little Pigs*). Each group chooses a book and decides how to share it. They are then charged with developing a book of poetry based on the chosen book. The poems do not have to simply retell the story. In fact, I encourage students to avoid a straight retelling of the story. Rather I ask them to base their poems on the ideas and characters that are presented in the book.

We talk about what types of books 7- and 8-year-olds like and what attracts children to books. We also talk about the different types of poems that would work well for a children's book. I share several examples of concrete poems and also provide formula poem formats (i.e., prepositional poem, septones, definition poems, adverb poems, cinquains, regulated cinquain, and so on). I also suggest that, considering the age of the intended readers, the books should be durable and should not use cursive writing or calligraphy, since these might be difficult for young readers to decipher.

Then I turn the students loose. Typically, they have five days to work on their books. The first day is spent sharing the book (this is usually done orally with each member taking turns reading) and fleshing out their ideas. Days two and three are spent developing ideas, collaborating on poems, sharing, and revising. The assignment only requires that the students write three different poems. However, it is a rare project that is turned in with only three poems—most of the books have between five and six.

I provide basic supplies for the students: glue, hot glue gun, binding machine and materials, rings to bind books, markers, crayons, water color paints, tape, scissors, etc. The students bring in any other supplies they need.

Each year the books become more and more elaborate. In year one, most of the books were made from construction paper and poster board. The following year, students began adding fabric (the Clothing and Design teacher allowed my students access to all the remnants and scraps her class had discarded), sequins, fabric paint, felt, etc. The first year, I received a book shaped like a llama, based on the book *Is Your Mama a Llama?* Since then I have received books shaped like peaches (*James and the Giant Peach*), fish, guitars, frogs (*The Frog Prince*), butterflies (*I Wish I Were a Butterfly*), pigs (*The True Story of the Three Little Pigs*), houses, lockers, trains, pizza slices (*Something Queer in the Cafeteria*), and in many other shapes. The books come in all sizes—some are tiny, some are oversized, and some ambitious students have even made pop-up books. (At the beginning of the project, I bring to class *How to Make Pop-Up Books* and *How to Make Super Pop-Up Books*, both written by Joan Irvine and published by William Morris, for interested students to consult.)

When the books are finished, I take them to local grammar schools where they are always well received by both teachers and, of course, the children. Usually, students in the receiving classes write thank-you notes to my students and tell us what they liked about the books.

I have always used this as a year-end project, but it could be incorporated earlier in the school year and extended by arranging a field trip where the authors would be able to present their books in person to their audience. I know this project is successful because every year I find it more and more difficult to part with the finished products. They are *incredible!*

Eileen Brusek-Kaczmarek, Whitney Young High School, Chicago, Illinois

Hands Inspire Descriptive Writing

This idea was given to me by Judith Kocela, a wonderful teacher at Stuyvesant High School in New York City. It is an effective way to give students experience with description and detail in their writing. I use this exercise with my ninth-grade English class.

Ask students to close their eyes and put their heads down on their desks. When they are quiet, ask them to imagine a person they know very well. Ask each student to bring up a vivid mental picture of the chosen person—what the person looks like, what the person is wearing, whether the person is sitting or standing, and finally, the person's hands.

Ask students to look closely at the person's hands. What do they look like? What do they feel like? Are they cold or warm? Long nails or short? Soft or rough? Are there scars, moles, or other marks on the person's hands? Let these questions float around the room and allow the students time to imagine their person's hands in vivid detail. After about two minutes, ask the students to lift their heads and, without talking, write a complete description of the person's hands. When they have written their description, ask the students to write a short story about what the person's hands are doing and then, at the end of the story, have the person notice them watching and say something to them.

Students may choose anyone they know well as a subject. However, I've found that ninth graders are consumed with thoughts of girlfriends, boyfriends, and crushes, and many students write detailed descriptions of the hands of their beloved. Students really enjoy this exercise, and I think it's partly because it gives them time to think about a special person while they are in class. Student also begin to understand the value of close observation and of precise detail in their writing.

Tara Restivo, Bergenfield High School, Bergenfield, New Jersey

Create a Menu

A number of us in our English Department have enjoyed using the following menu assignment as a way for students to demonstrate their creativity and their use of adjectives.

Student Guidelines

An interesting motif, tantalizing food described and pictured on an attractive menu, and delectable cooking—that is what makes a restaurant an excellent place to eat. This is your chance to create your own restaurant and its menu of inviting dishes.

Menus use a variety of intriguing adjectives for the kinds of food a restaurant serves, the service it provides, and the description of the dining establishment itself.

Directions

1. Choose a *food theme* for your restaurant. It could be Southern, French, Mexican, sports, the 1950s or any other theme you choose. Carry out the theme in the restaurant's name, the types of food offered, and the menu design.
2. Decide upon the types of food and the categories of dishes to be offered, such as appetizers, salads, entrees, à la carte (side dishes), desserts, and beverages. You should have at least *three to four food items* in each category of your choice.
3. Describe each dish using vivid, lively adjectives designed to entice a person to try the food item. Use a wide variety of adjectives. Do this in a phrase or sentence describing the food under the name of the food item.

4. The menu needs to be original. Design your own artwork and make your menu as colorful and interesting as possible.
5. The text inside the menu may be typed or printed with a computer.
6. Make the menu as professional as possible. Some factors to consider are visual appeal, originality, readability, neatness, spelling, and punctuation.
7. Each page has specific requirements:
   - The *front page* shows the name, location, and theme design and may also include a slogan, descriptive phrases, and other related information.
   - For the *interior pages,* divide the food into appropriate courses for your particular kind of restaurant (appetizers, salads, entrees, side dishes, desserts, beverages).
   - Name each dish, using mouth-watering adjectives, and briefly describe each dish in a sentence or two under the name.
   - Be selective! The quality of the work is more important than the quantity.
   - The pages listing menu items may have typed or computer printed descriptions neatly glued onto them.
   - The back page may have a choice of related writings: the history of the restaurant, a related child's game, endorsements from famous people who have eaten there, or something from your own creative imagination.
8. Reminders:
   - Your ideas should be original. Do not copy an existing restaurant's menu.
   - When your rough draft is completed, you'll receive several sheets of art paper to use for your final product.
   - Be sure to include prices for the various food items.

Carol Schowalter, El Roble Intermediate School, Claremont, California

Student Transformations à la *The Metamorphosis*

"When Gregor Samsa woke one morning after unsettling dreams he found himself changed into a monstrous vermin."

I ask my junior and senior College Literature students to become familiar with the above quotation. As it is one of the odder opening lines in world literature and a nice example of the technique of "shock" employed by many modern artists, I figure it's worth committing to student memories. As a class we discuss the novella in detail—talking of various critical interpretations of *The Metamorphosis,* as well as the students' own interpretations of what Kafka was trying to accomplish with this dark modern tale of salesman-turned-cockroach. Towards the end of our class interaction with *The Metamorphosis,* I challenge the students to create a metamorphosis. The assignment is simple (especially after reading and responding to several examples of professional criticism on Kafka's work).

Students are asked to write a page about some sort of transformation: *some* human must turn at *some* certain moment into something *else.* The character could be waking up, like Gregor, or driving her car home from work, in the lunch line at school, at the grocery story, in a swimming pool—anywhere. The character merely needs to metamorphose into something, *anything* else, as long as it isn't "a monstrous vermin."

Due to the brevity of this one-page assignment, I tell the students they may spend the entire length of their paper merely discussing what the character has become and his/her/its initial response to the change, or they could offer, as Kafka does (but in an abbreviated version for the assignment) a display of the response of not only the character, but also his employer, family members, significant other(s), etc. The students were invited, if they preferred, to take the character in an accelerated manner to its final unfortunate demise or re-transformation. We shared the responses via a reading table, and later I read several of their tales aloud to the class.

The students turned their human characters into a variety of critters and objects: a sea lion, a clucking chicken, a kitten, a crow, a piece of paper, a balloon, and, on the more repulsive end of the spectrum, a "booger" and a "turd." Some of the pieces were written in first person, but most were written in a limited third-person fashion, as is Kafka's *The Metamorphosis.*

Below are segments of the most interesting of the student products:

John, a senior, discusses an isolated individual as a victim of the technological age:

"Jeff Johnson woke up one morning and found himself

changed into a gigantic microwave: a big box with buttons, a door, and a cord." His voice was a "buzzing hum." Jeff tried so hard to leave the bedroom to go to school that he damaged his cord. "His dad was so mad he broke through the door, saw Jeff, ran to the kitchen to grab some TV dinners. He threw them at Jeff, broke his glass door and killed him."

William, also a senior, offers another German "bug" version:

"Segory Gramsa woke from unsettling dreams to find he had been changed into a Volkswagon Bug. His bed had been smashed from the weight . . . his voice sounded like a horn . . . as he thought about moving, his engine sputtered to life."

Miranda's first-person version focuses on specific problems and the possible neglect and death following the change:

"One morning I woke up and found out that I had been changed into a big potted plant, a peace lily in fact. As I lay in bed, I realized that I would never again be able to go to work or school or even on a date. I came to the conclusion that I had to inform my family of what had happened. I tried to roll myself from bed, and when I finally succeeded, my soil spilled out onto the floor and my pot cracked. My family heard the noise and came running. When they finally opened the door and saw what had happened they were shocked. They cleaned me up and set me in the corner of my room. They never came in to water me, never opened the windows to let in the sunshine and fresh air, and eventually I withered away from neglect and loss of love."

Josh, a junior, employed the postmodern technique of *shock*—taking risks in topic and character. "I woke from unsettling dreams as a woman—what will this mean? I have breasts. Should I have children?"

Another junior, Matt, found his human character turned into "a blank white sheet of paper, which happens to be the one I am writing on right now. And every time I write on this paper it is as if he were being stabbed with a dull knife, and the letters that appear—what you think is ink—is actually his blood."

Finally, Shawna's first-person character acquiesces, as does Gregor, to the desires of the family, although sacrificing her own freedom:

> "While walking home from a friend's house one day I looked down and saw that I had no feet. I looked for my hands and instead I found beautiful butterfly wings. I flew to my house and saw my dad outside grilling. I fluttered around his head. He ran inside yelling to my mother that he had found the most beautiful butterfly ever. He came out a second later with a jar. It was not hard to catch me; I didn't try to fly away. Now I sit in the living room looking out the window."

Kafka's incredible imagination and bizarre tale seem to cry for response; hence, I will continue to encourage the students to write their own "variations of change" after encountering and considering the plight of Gregor Samsa.

Tracy Anderson Tensen, Southeast Polk High School, Runnells, Iowa

Modern-Day Rip Van Winkles

In my eleventh-grade English class our focus is on American literature. During our short story unit my classes often read and discuss "Rip Van Winkle." About midway through the story I present the following, which is one of my most successful and popular assignments.

Students are told the unthinkable has happened: They fell asleep in my English class and slept for twenty years! Their assignment is to write a short story about this event. The minimum requirements are as follows:

- two typed or three handwritten pages in short story form
- parallels to "Rip Van Winkle"
  —details of physical changes in their bodies, the landscape, and society
  —a description of how the student gradually realized what had happened
  —at least a few lines of dialogue (for which we review how to write conversation with correct paragraphing and punctuation marks)
- either a serious or humorous tone may be used

Many students are surprised by their own creativity. Some have illustrated their stories. I have also discovered that students are usually divided between optimism (revitalization of the city, healthier attitudes, etc.) and pessimism (increased homeless population, wars, etc.) in their view of their society twenty years into the future. In some of their stories computers have replaced the teachers and administration. Other stories have robots doing hall and cafeteria duty. In some stories, students wake up and wonder why I would let them sleep for so long!

This is an assignment I truly look forward to reading and grading.

Valerie Gagg Beaudreau, E. C. Goodwin Regional Vocational-Technical High School, New Britain, Connecticut

Dearest Abigail: Writing a Colonist's Letter

What makes people choose sides in a conflict?

When the American colonists were in conflict with King George, what side would your students have taken? Would they have been Patriots, Loyalists, or would they have chosen to be uninvolved and neutral?

In this project, students examine the reasons the colonists made the decisions they did and consider what decisions they would have made if they had lived during the 1770s. Students take on the personae of fictional persons living in the American colonies at the time of the Revolutionary War and write letters to friends or relatives, expressing their point of view about the conflict. This strategy can be effective in a core curriculum setting, with a teaching team, or used as an interdisciplinary approach.

First, the students are divided into groups of four. Each group is given a piece of chart paper and four markers of different colors. The group is assigned a position—Patriot, Loyalist, or neutral. The group brainstorms reasons why an individual would choose this position and lists the reasons on the paper. (Each student in the group uses a different-colored marker so that everyone's comments can be seen at a glance.) The students should be encouraged to include the reasons they've studied in history class, but also should include personal reasons why someone might choose a particular position. For example, Patriots could choose this side because of a desire for representation or to avoid heavy taxes imposed by the King. This position might also be chosen because Patriots find the idea of rebellion to be exciting, because they want to leave home and have a war adventure, or maybe because they wish to defy the Loyalist position of their fathers.

Next, the students create their fictional selves and write a letter to a friend or relative. Some possible personae are: a soldier fighting with General Washington, a teenage girl whose family life has been disrupted by war, a young boy who desires the adventure of fighting a war, a shop owner who experiences the effects of high taxation, a mother whose husband and son disagree about the conflict. Students are encouraged to imagine what life would be like for the person they invent and to look at the situation from their character's point of view.

A letter should include the following:

- One's position on the conflict, supported by reasons for one's position.
- Reference to real historical events (for example, the Battle of Lexington and Concord, Paul Revere's ride, the occurrence of the quartering of British soldiers in people's homes, etc.).
- Pieces of family and local news and gossip.
- Letter format, including a heading with a town and colony and a date.

Ellen Brosnahan, Haines Middle School, St. Charles, Illinois

A Civil War Story Sparks Historical Writing

Rich with exquisite illustrations and a writing style that evokes a sense of history, Patricia Polacco's *Pink and Say* (Philomel Books, 1994) retells a story, passed down from her great-grandfather, about how his life was saved during the Civil War by a brave young black soldier, Pinkus Aylee. *Pink and Say* is an enjoyable book to read aloud in the classroom, and a natural starting point for discussion, writing, and historical research.

Begin by reading *Pink and Say* aloud and sharing the illustrations with the class. Emphasize that the book is not merely about fighting or political issues. Rather, it is about the emotions and inner conflicts of people in a country torn apart by war. The conflict exists not only between the North and South but also between mothers and sons; pacifists and nonpacifists; and soldiers and the families left behind to defend themselves and run family businesses.

Potential activities for reading and writing connections using *Pink and Say* include the following:

(1) Students can conduct interviews relating to the Civil War. Students who can trace their family histories back to Civil War times may research their family geneologies and interview family members for what they know. Other students can find neighbors and friends to interview, or can research families living at that time and create fictional interviews based in fact. Pertinent information might include:

- if and when the family emigrated to America and where they settled;
- which side of the war the family supported;
- the reason for the family's affiliation with one side or the other;
- details that provide a sense of the family's daily life; such as how they made their living, typical food and clothing, family customs, religious practices, and so on.

Teachers can use this information as a mini-lesson to compare and contrast differing views. Be sure to provide students with the freedom for embellishing factual data with fiction, as there are certain to be many details unknown to the person being interviewed or unavailable to the student doing research.

(2) Students can explore the inner conflicts of people living in America during the Civil War by:

- writing a letter from the viewpoint of a young soldier corresponding to his mother, wife, child, or other family member;
- writing a letter from the viewpoint of a person writing to a family member fighting in the war;
- writing a Civil War journal from the viewpoint of a soldier, recalling the day-to-day accounts of battles and his reactions to the fighting.

(3) Students can assume the identity of a child their age during the Civil War by:

- creating a dialogue about how the war has affected their daily lives;
- writing a letter to a child in another country, explaining why America is fighting a civil war.

The author of *Pink and Say* has attempted to re-create dialects so that the dialogue sounds authentic. In the following example, taken from near the beginning of the story, the narrator, Sheldon Curtis ("Say") is first found by Pinkus Aylee where he lies wounded in a field.

"Bein' here, boy, means you gotta be dead," the voice said as he gave me a drink from his kit. "Where you hit? 'Cause if it's a belly hit, I gotta leave you here," he said.

I had never seen a man like him so close before. His skin was the color of polished mahogany. He was flyin' Union colors like me. My age, maybe. His voice was soothin' and his help was good.

"Hit in the leg," I told him. "Not bad if it don't go green."

"Can you put weight on it?" he asked as he pulled me to my feet. "We gotta keep movin.' If we stay in one spot, marauders will find us. They're ridin' drag and lookin' for wounded."

As an enrichment activity, students could try rewriting their dialogues or letters so that they speak as young people might have during the Civil War. These dialogues would be great fun for students to read aloud to the class, or perhaps perform as a skit.

Many fine novels and stories based in this time period are available, both contemporary and classic. Choose *The Red Badge of Courage, Little Women,* or *The Glory Field* as your core novel, and let *Pink and Say* function as the introduction. Other possible resources with a Civil War theme include:

- *Letters from a Slave Girl: The Story of Harriet Jacobs* by Mary E. Lyons
- *Cecil's Story* by George Ella Lyon
- *Bull Run* by Paul Fleischman
- *Behind the Blue and Gray: The Soldier's Life in the Civil War* by Delia Ray
- *Across Five Aprils* by Irene Hunt

Kathy Hughes, Annunciation Orthodox School, Houston, Texas

A Metaphorical Introduction to the Writing Process

For years I have looked for an effective hands-on activity which would introduce my students to the entire writing process in a single class period. However, I wanted an activity outside of writing itself. I needed a "bucket" which would hold all the concepts I teach within the writing process: critic/creator, audience, purpose, rehearsal, revision, editing, publishing. Finally I came up with the metaphor of sculpting.

I asked my students to make or purchase one can of colored Play-Doh. I blocked my class with my history team-teacher so that I could have two full periods. Students were paired with response partners nearby, with whom they traded opinions at certain points during the activity. Following my script (included here), I asked my students to design a pencil holder for their desks. My purpose was to teach new writing concepts and terms as they worked through each phase of the creative process.

As students generated many ideas in the presculpting phase, I talked about diverse ways to acquire ideas and the initial questions writers ask themselves about audience, purpose, point of view, and tone. I forced them to squish already structured ideas and find others, emphasizing that writers, like sculptors, try many ideas before focusing on one. As they labored through first drafts, I stressed the importance of making meaning, of developing a single idea, and introduced the concept of unity.

Peer response became important now, and students brainstormed questions they would ask each other as they tried to improve their products. The questions were similar in all six of my classes. Is this piece functional? Is it creative? Can you tell what it is? What shall I do to improve it? Thus we entered the revision stage, and students looked at their pieces again from many different points of view. What works, I asked? What doesn't work? What needs to be redefined? These are the revision questions of writers and sculptors. Fingers were busy.

The editing stage witnessed students checking details, smoothing out surfaces, straightening up edges—just as one might finetune a piece of writing by checking spelling and punctuation. Chunks of Play-Doh in different colors were exchanged as students added last-minute touches to make their pieces look good. Students wandered around the room, commenting and advising other artists. Pieces were then titled, displayed, and evaluated.

The next day, I asked my students to write me a quick draft describing the writing process. Without notes or books, they generated key words and concepts, and explained in great detail the process of a writer. One student wrote, "I am a writer, a sculptor of words into form. I rehearse, make meaning, and improve."

For parents' open house, I had 150 multicolored pencil holders spread over the desks, window ledges, and tables. Each proudly bore a title and an artist's name.

Throughout the year now, I call my students sculptors, and they know it's true. The learning is locked in their fingers!

Here is the "script" I use to walk my students' through the metaphor process.

Script for Using Play-Doh to Teach the Writing Process

Today's lesson requires no pencil or paper, only your hands. While you work with your hands, please listen to me. It is important that you connect what you are doing with what I am saying.

From this activity today, you will be able to answer these questions: What process does a writer go through to produce a final piece? How is a writer like a sculptor? [I write these questions on the board to help students focus.]

To get ready, clear your desks and take out your Play-Doh and a pencil.

Close your eyes and get the feel of the clay in your hands. S*l*o*w*l*y knead the dough. A writer must know the material before using it in a final piece. That's why it is important for you to read a variety of books and explore the dictionary and the thesaurus. These are places you find the material of writers.

What is the material of writers? Words! It is important that you play with words, experiment with words in journals or learning logs or letters or notes. A writer plays with words like a sculptor kneads clay. Take a few minutes now and play. See what this material can do. Stretch it. Pile it. Press it. Fold it. Don't make anything out of it. Just play. [I continue speaking while students do this.]

In a minute I am going to ask you to design something, but before I do, I want to introduce you to two parts of you whom you may not know. A writer, like a sculptor, has two parts that work together to produce a final piece. These two parts we call the *creator* and the *critic*. Which do you think has a bigger part in the first stages of writing or sculpting? It's the creator, the uncensored part, the part of you that envisions ideas, that brainstorms possibilities, and conceives of all sorts of ways to do something.

When do you suppose the critic starts to work? Your critic part jumps up when you need to decide, when you need to analyze, revise or edit, when a judgment call is needed. If you hear a voice starting to judge when you are still in the prewriting stages, when you are still just getting ideas for your writing, *tell that voice to be quiet and wait for his or her turn.*

Today you will create something. You will put it on display for other students and their parents to see. So your audience is more than just you or me. Your audience is all other students and parents. It is important to know who your audience is before you begin, because knowing your audience can affect what you create.

You cannot begin until you know what your purpose is, just as a writer cannot begin to write until she knows what her purpose is, why she is writing. Today your purpose is to create a pencil holder—something that will hold a pencil on your desk. A purpose focuses our intentions. It sets a path, a destination.

I want you to start to create the first of many ideas you will come up with for a pencil holder. Don't decide the final product yet. Just experiment with lots of ideas. Listen while you work.

A writer always has a purpose. It may be to describe something, or to explain something, or to tell a story. Sometimes the purpose may just be to get rid of anger or sadness—just to put things down on paper that the writer can't say aloud. Sometimes a writer may write to persuade. Other times a writer's purpose might be to give information, like explaining to someone how to print a document on the computer or how to get from your house to school. A writer may write to explore how he feels about something. His purpose may be to find out what he thinks.

Okay, mush up your dough, and start again. I know you don't like destroying your first creation, but I want to prove to you that there are thousands more ideas where that one came from. What part of you came up with that first design? That's right, your creator, and your creator is anxious to give you more ideas. Start another design. As you do, please listen.

The creative process has many stages. As a sculptor, the one you are experiencing right now might be called *presculpting*. In writing, it is called *prewriting* or *rehearsing*. It is the time when you are getting ideas and putting them together in new ways, preparing for the final production. During this stage only your creator is at work. Your critic is asleep. For some of you, your critic wants to come out and judge, judge, judge. Tell your critic politely to be quiet. As you rehearse, keep in mind your *purpose*. Ask yourself, "What am I trying to accomplish? How do I want my audience to feel?" This will keep you focused.

Now mush that idea and start again. Take a couple of minutes to try something new and different from your last design. [I allow students a couple of minutes to start again.]

Okay, now mush it up. Let's start again. But before you do, let's discuss what it is you want to achieve in this piece, because we are getting ready to do a first draft. What criteria shall we use to judge this piece? [At this point we spend a few minutes talking about how we want to judge the pieces. My students' comments always lead eventually to the ideas of beauty (aesthetics; sensory appeal; is it pleasing to look at or touch?), function (usefulness; practicality; does it do what it was intended to?), and creativity (originality; imaginativeness; does it surprise or amuse you?). I write the criteria we come up with on the board.]

Keep these criteria in mind as you design. This time will be your last. Let your critic help you pick out your best idea or combine your ideas to create an entirely new pencil holder. This last design will be your first draft of your final piece. You have five minutes. Please work in silence. [I let students know when there is one minute remaining in the work time.]

You have finished your first draft. A writer, like a sculptor, thinks about how the audience will respond to his or her work. The writer, like the sculptor, may stop at any point and get response from other people. Ask your partner to look at your design and tell you if he or she knows where the pencil will go. This will show that you have given your form meaning. It is not just a lot of Play-Doh thrown together— it has one idea or purpose. This quality is often called *unity*. This one idea should be obvious to your response partner. If not, you haven't focused your ideas clearly enough.

You have now gone through two stages of the writing process: 1) rehearsals to come up with lots of ideas and 2) a first draft to get the essential meaning. Now let's move on to the revision stage.

Revision literally means *to see again*. So, I want you to look at your pencil holder from various points of view. This will help you see it in a new way. Then you can decide what you want to do to it. So stand on your chair or look at it from a distance. What do you see that you would like to change or refine? Now get in front of your desk and stoop down close. What do you want to change or refine? Now look at it from the side. Now from the other side. Now sit down.

You have looked at what needs to be refined. There will never be a time in your writing when you can't revise—even up until the end. Some people are still revising while they edit or while typing their final draft. That's because every time we reread our writing or "re-view" our pencil holders, we will "re-see" it and come up with a better way of saying or designing it.

One of the ways you can revise is to do what you just did—look at your work from another point of view or have someone else read it and comment. So right now, let your partner look at it, and then listen to his or her ideas for improving it. You don't have to take your partner's suggestions, but think about them, and make any revisions that you think will improve your pencil holder. [Students confer and revise briefly.]

Now you are ready to begin the final stage—editing. At this point a writer looks closely at details such as spelling, punctuation, and capitalization, which help make the writing clear and readable. Since this is detail work, trade a little colored Play-Doh with your partner or someone nearby so that you can add any necessary finishing touches to your pencil holder. [I allow a few minutes here.]

The details you just added are only finishing touches. You could have a lot of nice little details on your pencil holder, but if it doesn't have meaning, if it doesn't have unity and hold together, these finishing touches aren't worth anything. The same is true for writing. Good spelling, punctuation, and usage are only important if the piece itself has meaning, unity, and coherence.

Now admire your product. A writer is like a sculptor. A writer, like a sculptor, like you today, goes through a process involving many changes which leads to a final product.

Give your final product a name. Write the name on a 3" x 5" card, set your pencil holder on the card, and display it. A writer is like a sculptor, sharing his or her work with the public. Put your final product on display so all can see.

Let's walk around the room quietly looking at each masterpiece. Please keep comments to yourself right now. [We review the final products.]

Now it is time for comments: Look at your partner's piece. Pick one positive comment you would like to use to admire the piece aloud. Stand up and tell the class. And let's applaud each sculptor/writer.

Rosemary Faucette, Fayetteville, Arkansas

Are You More Like . . . ?

The following list of comparisons works well as a prewriting exercise; it produces interesting images and starting points for further prose or poetry writing.

This is my own variation; I'm not sure who deserves credit for the original idea. It was passed on to me when I began teaching in 1974 and I've used it successfully ever since.

I ask students to respond quickly to the list and then choose one comparison for more thoughtful consideration and elaboration. The results of the other comparions can be saved, sifted through, and developed into longer writings at a later time.

Are you more like . . .

- breakfast or dinner?
- summer or winter?
- the country or the city?
- the present or the future?
- the tortoise or the hare?
- a Hyundai or a Lexus?
- patent leather or suede?
- a paddle or a ping-pong ball?
- an electric typewriter or a ballpoint pen?
- a clothesline or a kite string?
- a rock band or a string quartet?
- a fly swatter or fly paper?
- a file cabinet or a liquor cabinet?
- a mountain or a valley?
- "a stitch in time" or "better late than never"?
- a screened patio or a picture window?
- a babbling brook or a placid lake?
- Niagara Falls or Mount St. Helens?
- a motorcycle or a tricycle?
- a roller skate or a pogo stick?
- yellow or blue?
- fire or water?
- earth or air?

After you've responded to all of the above, choose one comparison and explain, in detail, why you answered the way you did.

Carolyn Adamson, Ruben S. Ayala High School, Chino Hills, California

The Short Story: Where to Begin?

When I used to teach tenth-grade English, one of our writing assignments was a short story. I struggled with this. I wanted to teach it as a *process,* but I wasn't sure what the approved process for writing a short story was.

"How should we start?" the students asked.

"I don't know," I replied.

Assuming that all stories begin with a sentence, I decided we might as well start there. I brought a bunch of my favorite novels and short stories to class the next day and spent the entire class period reading the first sentences aloud. After each one, we talked about whether we liked it or not. For example:

> "Solomon carried Livvie twenty-one miles from her home when her married her." ("Livvie," Eudora Welty)

> "She was a large woman with a purse that had everything in it but hammer and nails." ("Thank You, M'am," Langston Hughes)

> "It was a bright cold day in April, and the clocks were striking thirteen." (*1984,* George Orwell)

> "When Miss Emily Grierson died, our whole town went to her funeral: the men through a sort of respectful affection for a fallen monument, the women mostly out of curiosity to see the inside of her house, which no one save an old manservant—a combined gardener and cook—had seen in at least ten years." ("A Rose for Emily," William Faulkner)

> "It was a dark and stormy night." (*A Wrinkle in Time,* Madeleine L'Engle)

> "Besides the neutral expression that she wore when she was alone, Mrs. Freeman had two others, forward and reverse, that she used for all her human dealings." ("Good Country People," Flannery O'Connor)

> "The sky above the port was the color of television, tuned to a dead channel." (*Neuromancer,* William Gibson)

We talked about the different styles—how some writers were more descriptive; how others jumped into the action of the story in such a

way that you *had* to read the next sentence; how some writers included details that foreshadowed events to come; how others revealed character.

At the end of the hour, I told the class to go home and write one sentence—a really good sentence to start a story with.

"But what should the story be about?" they asked.

"Who cares?" I answered. "Just write one good sentence. Is that too much to ask?"

Here are some of the sentences they wrote:

"I had never shot a gun before."

"The Porters never really were a part of society."

"The phone did not ring, therefore I must answer it. Goodbye."

"Two down, one to go."

"The gun fell to the floor."

"How can you not appreciate the firm roundness of those buns?"

"I was there, there when they came."

"The television and the lights in the room snapped off in unison as a jagged bolt of lightning struck the telephone pole."

"The clothes lay strewn across the floor."

I wrote one too:

> "Ray Bob had no way of knowing that in a little building on the other side of the cement plant they were testing sperm."

The next day we devoted the class period to listening to (and discussing) each other's sentences. Needless to say, the next assignment was to complete the story. Students' efforts were wildly uneven, but on balance the stories were pretty good. I'm not willing to say this is the best (or even a good) method for teaching short story writing, but I think the assignment advances several worthwhile goals:

- Students think consciously about introductions. I think we can develop skills through this activity that might transfer to other genres and types of writing.
- Students are exposed very quickly to a wide variety of literature and literary styles. Granted, they are only hearing the first sentence read aloud, but they can listen to and appreciate one sentence of a story that might otherwise be impenetrable to them.
- Students begin the process of fiction writing in a non-threatening manner.
- Students offer and receive peer response within a non-threatening climate.

I don't think we should teach fiction writing in high school as an end in itself. I don't, for example, think creative work by high school students should be evaluated the way we might evaluate other types of writing. But I do think creative writing is a powerful way to develop enthusiasm about language and story, and I think we can connect many of the skills students might learn by writing fiction to other more traditional types of writing.

For what it's worth, I finished my story too. And I'll bet you'd like to find out what happened.

F. Todd Goodson, East Carolina University

2   Literature

Reading and responding to literature, students explore universal issues of human nature as well as the more personal issues that spring from their own experiences, thoughts, and emotions. The varied ideas in this section further students' exploration of literature in many different ways: students use popular music to learn about allusion, review a novel through collaborative illustration, translate their understanding of a reading into script form, and respond to Robert Cormier's short stories by interviewing relatives and neighbors about their teenage years.

Reviewing a Novel through Collaborative Illustration

This activity takes about two days and works well as a test review, particularly at the middle school and junior high levels. Students appreciate the fact that it provides a break after reading a major work.

Materials needed are pencils, markers, colored pencils, or crayons; and large sheets of white paper (approximately 3 ft. x 4 ft.).

Roll paper works best for this activity and can be cut to the desired size. If necessary, you can buy it inexpensively at a school supply store (I've found 20-foot rolls for $2).

Divide the class into groups of four. Have group members list, on a blank sheet of paper, the six most important events in any given story. (I use this at the end of reading *Romeo and Juliet* and *The Crucible*.) When students have the six events listed, I ask them to divide the large sheet of roll paper into six equal squares and draw the events they have chosen in the six squares on their paper. Students are encouraged to discuss the events together and work out the way they will depict them. I encourage each one of the group members to be working at all times.

Some students may complain that they can't draw well enough or that there isn't enough room for everyone to be working at the same time; I just tell them that any style of sketching or diagramming is okay, and that they will need to cooperate to figure out a way to get it done. Students are encouraged to devise whatever system best works for their group, whether it's assigning squares to individuals, using an assembly-line system, or all tackling one square at a time and then moving on to the next. Often students spread themselves out on the floor or in the hallway to allow themselves more room to work.

At the end of the second day, with 10 minutes left of class, I have them present their six events to the rest of the class. Some events are the same across groups, but the drawings themselves are always unique and the oral presentations often emphasize events differently. I haven't ever added this twist, but I have thought about having the class vote on the one they like best and offering to keep it up on the wall during the test.

I'd recommend *not* telling students that they will be drawing the six events while they are initially listing them on paper. That way students do not limit themselves by what they feel they can or cannot draw.

An alternative to this method is to have students draw and then cut out the characters from large, colored roll paper and add details to each character as they read along. For example, in *The Crucible,* students might create a character cut-out of John Proctor and then add a symbol of the adultery commandment, or create a cut-out of Mary Warren and add a bird. In *Romeo and Juliet,* the students might add a ring and a dagger to Juliet as they read along, or a vial of poison and a Bible to Friar Lawrence.

Each of these ideas will let students exercise their imagination while focusing their attention on the characters and events of the story or novel under discussion.

Kelly A. Wolslegel, Preble High School, Green Bay, Wisconsin

Introducing Students to Genre: Converting Memories to Fiction

I've found what I think is an effective way to have students discover the technical differences in genres, something I had never felt successful in teaching. Instead of using only the short stories in the class anthology, I began with autobiographies. I included an excerpt of Zora Neale Hurston's autobiography *Dust Tracks in the Road,* in which she describes herself as a child sitting on the gatepost accosting strangers who drove by her house. My 10th graders then wrote

their own "memoir" of some incident in their young lives, which they read to the class and discussed.

Later, we read Hurston's short story "Isis," which is a fictionalized version of the same gatepost incident she mentions in her autobiography. I asked students in groups to list the major differences between Hurston's autobiographical version and her fictionalized version of the story.

The natural follow-up to this was a conversion of their own memoirs to a piece of fiction. Students' completed fiction pieces demonstrated a deeper grasp of literary elements than first-quarter sophomores had ever displayed. Incidentally, students not only had fun and learned a great deal about genre, but an unexpected bonus was the building of a tremendous sense of classroom community from hearing and responding to each others' true stories.

I continued this tack when introducing drama, but instead of having students read a play and determining how drama is different from short stories and essays, I asked students in groups to take one of their fiction stories per group and turn it into a play. I felt that by actually having to think about what changes were needed, they might be more inclined to notice and remember the elements of a play when they read one. This proved to be a successful activity, and after writing scripts and performing their own "plays," students were ready to watch for dramatic elements when we began our drama unit.

Carol Zuccaro, St. Johnsbury Academy, St. Johnsbury, Vermont

Multicultural Book Collage

I teach in a large suburban district in which the majority of the students are white and come from upper-middle-class families. Although many are well-traveled, most have limited experiences with people of other ethnic backgrounds. To encourage my seventh-grade students to learn more about other cultures, I assign a multicultural book project.

I begin by talking a little bit about the word "multicultural" to get the students thinking about culture and its importance in our lives. Next, I bring in a wide selection of multicultural books from the media center. I also pull books from my shelves and display them around the room. I give a brief booktalk for each and then allow students to select books to read. I usually give the students about three weeks to read their books.

While they are reading, the students keep journals. I give them a list of questions and ask that each student have five entries by the time he or she is finished. The questions are meant to elicit thinking about culture and the similarities and differences between the students' lives and the lives of the characters. Below is a partial list of questions I provide to stimulate the students' thinking and writing.

Journal Questions

- What connections are there between the book and your own life?
- What is the author saying about life and living in your book?
- How have your views changed after reading this book?
- What has this book helped you to understand more fully?
- What cultural differences are there between you and the main character in this book?
- Although the main character and you are from different cultures, what similarities exist between the two of you?
- What fascinates you about the culture(s) presented in this book?
- What are the differences in the educational process as experienced by the character in this book and as experienced by you?
- What is the main conflict in this book? Is it internal or external? In

what way does the culture presented in this book affect the conflict or problem?

- If you were the main character in this book, how would you have handled the conflict or problem?

Each student also fills in a Venn diagram as he or she reads. The left side is labeled with the student's name, and the right side is labeled with the main character's name. The differences between the student and the character are listed in their respective circles. Where the circles overlap, the student lists similarities.

Creating Collages

When the students have finished reading their books, writing their journal entries, and filling in their Venn diagrams, they are ready to create their collages. The students use poster board; clippings from magazines, catalogs, and brochures; photographs; and sometimes three-dimensional objects in creating their collages. The students must clearly demonstrate the connections made between the books and their lives. They must address the similarities and the differences between themselves and the main characters in their books. The items should represent aspects of culture, but I also allow other artifacts. The title of the book along with the author's name must also be clearly visible. Some students have chosen to create collages shaped as Venn diagrams. Others have taken their collages and shaped them into symbols of importance to their books. For example, one student who read *Journey of the Sparrows* by Fran Leeper Buss arranged her pictures, words, and clippings into the shape of a bird. Another student, after reading *Roll of Thunder, Hear My Cry* by Mildred D. Taylor, cut a large circle from a poster board and divided it into three pieces, two sections for differences and one for similarities.

Students then present their collages to the class. Students begin by introducing themselves. They must address the similarities and the differences between themselves and the main characters, the main conflict in the book, and the theme. I also want them to share with the class what they learned and/or what they found fascinating about the cultures. These carefully crafted, colorful collages are then posted around the room and in the hallways for others to appreciate.

My students find they have much in common with their peers from other cultures. When they begin to relate to the characters in their books, their interest in reading increases. Many books go unread until they are introduced and students have had a chance to read, understand, and share their understanding with their classmates. The most effective motivator is the other students in class who have read these books and are excited about what they have read.

Scott Slomsky, Liberty Junior School, Middletown, Ohio

Connecting and Reflecting

One of the units that my ninth-grade students really enjoy is a three-week study of Robert Cormier's collection of short stories entitled *Eight Plus One*. Cormier wants high school students to realize that many teenagers face similar problems in their lives. In fact, these same problems were faced by their parents and grandparents when they were teenagers. In the introduction to *Eight Plus One*, Cormier explains the process that he used to write his short stories. First he begins with an emotion that he wants to convey and then he develops characters and a plot that evoke that emotion.

I use three activities with my students that help them to understand the relevance of these stories to their lives. I begin with an interview project. Each student interviews three people of different ages about what their teenage years were like. In class we brainstorm a list of questions to elicit information about a person's teenage experiences.

As students interview their parents, grandparents, aunts, or older brothers and sisters, they begin to realize that there are many common threads that run through everyone's experiences. Much to some students' surprise, their parents got into trouble in school, participated in sports, and argued with their siblings. This project gets teenagers talking with their parents. After completing the oral interviews, students write papers summarizing the information that they learned, comparing and contrasting the teenage problems and issues that they have faced with those faced by the people they interviewed.

The second writing project that I include in this unit involves daily journal writing. Each of the journal topics relates to a universal problem or issue that Cormier presents in one of his short stories. Students write in their journals for ten minutes during class or as a homework assignment. I encourage students to share these entries with each other. Again, students begin to make connections, this time between problems faced by Cormier's characters and problems that they themselves face. For example, journal topics for "The Moustache" would include topics such as aging grandparents, the loss of an older relative, or a visit to a nursing home.

The culminating activity of this unit is short story writing, using some of Robert Cormier's techniques as a model. Before beginning the story, students brainstorm a list of emotions that they have experienced, characters that might feel these emotions, and situations that evoke these emotions. I emphasize that the idea for their story must begin with an emotion. The other requirements of this story include the use of similes and metaphors, dialogue, and teenage characters who face a universal problem. I also ask that students create story titles that have symbolic meaning.

I find that my students not only enjoy reading and discussing Cormier's short stories, they also enjoy connecting and reflecting with each other and with their families around topics dealt with in these stories.

Susan Robertson, Danvers High School, Danvers, Massachusetts

Lyrics and Allusion

If music can soothe the savage beast, surely it can tame a roomful of tenth-grade English students. Well, okay, that's a bit much to expect from one song, but students do enjoy the change of pace that the use of music in the classroom brings; unfortunately, it's not always practical. I have found a way to teach the use of allusion to my sophomores that the students and I both enjoy and that gives them an opportunity to be creative.

The lesson starts with reading and discussing a poem (or short story) that is rich in allusions. I often use Anne Sexton's poem "Cinderella" for this exercise. During our discussion of the poem I define the term *allusion* for them and we pick out some of the many allusions that Sexton uses. The sophomore literature textbook that we use (*Elements of Literature: Fourth Course.* Holt, Rinehart, and Winston, 1989). includes Sexton's poem and identifies the allusions in footnotes. It may be more enjoyable and challenging for students if they read the poem first without such aids.

Students may be curious about such references as *from diapers to*

Dior, which *Elements of Literature* explains as "an allusion to a true story: a Danish maid married one of the rich Rockefeller sons."

Next, I have students get out a sheet of paper, and I ask them to listen to the tape I am about to play. They are to jot down every allusion they hear. I warn them that they will not get them all, but they should try to get as many as they can.

I then begin to play Billy Joel's song "We Didn't Start the Fire" from his *Storm Front* tape (CBS Records, 1989); every stanza is packed with allusions. I include the first stanza (of five) and the chorus here for reference.

> *Harry Truman, Doris Day, Red China, Johnnie Ray*
> *South Pacific, Walter Winchell, Joe DiMaggio*
> *Joe McCarthy, Richard Nixon, Studebaker, Television*
> *North Korea, South Korea, Marilyn Monroe*
> *Rosenbergs, H-bomb, Sugar Ray, Panmunjon*
> *Brando, The King and I, and the Catcher in the Rye*
> *Eisenhower, Vaccine, England's got a new queen*
> *Marciano, Liberace, Santayana goodbye*

> Chorus:
> *We didn't start the fire*
> *It was always burning*
> *Since the world's been turning*
> *We didn't start the fire*
> *No we didn't light it*
> *but we tried to fight it*

Some students immediately begin writing as fast as they can; others have to be encouraged to begin because they feel overwhelmed by the sheer number of allusions. When the song is finished, students count the allusions they caught on paper and the two or three with the most receive a small reward. I remind them that some of the allusions were to popular culture, which changes quickly, and were therefore no longer recognizable to them, and that this is why textbook editors often identify allusions (whether to popular culture, history, the Bible, or mythology) in footnotes.

I then place the students in groups of two or three. I have typed copies of the words to the song so that each group can look at them as they proceed to the next part of the lesson. I tell them that since the song originally came out about six or seven years ago, it needs updating. This becomes their group task: to compose two or three stanzas that reflect events of the past few years.

To accomplish this, first students need to brainstorm significant events, newsworthy people, and bits of popular culture memorable from their middle and high school years. From their brainstorming list, they determine what will be useful in their stanzas. I encourage them to use end rhyme, but because of time constraints, I do not expect them to use internal rhyme as Billy Joel did. Often, the students will ask me to play the song again for "inspiration" as they work; this also reinforces the rhythm of the lyrics.

Once students have their stanzas ready, I pass out orange flame-shaped paper for them to write their final drafts on. With our seventy-five minute class periods, we can usually accomplish at least this much in one class period. Sometimes the sharing, the most rewarding part, has to wait until the next day. Some groups will actually sing their lyrics, but most just read them aloud. The finished products are posted on the wall.

Here are a few examples written by my students:

Bill Clinton, Bob Dole, George Bush, Ross Perot
Tonya Harding, Susan Smith, Lorena Bobbitt didn't miss
Oklahoma, Waco, Bosnia, Castro
Forrest Gump, Lion King, Mr. Holland on the screen
Baseball strike, Super Bowl, Nolan Ryan is getting old
Michael Jackson and O.J., What else do I have to say!
    —Trisha Reed and Jennifer Brady

Dennis Miller, Calvin Klein, River Phoenix, cocaine lines,
Michael Irvin, Internet, Cindy Crawford, Valujet
Kurt Cobain, Chris Reeves, Doc Martens, hair weaves,
Cowboys in the Super Bowl, Bill Clinton, no control
Stephen King, Princess Di, O.J. trial, *Days of Our Lives,*
Mike Tyson, mad cows, Rodman is a bride now.
Magic Johnson, HIV, Hugh Grant, Pamela Lee,
Michael Jordan, baseball, Bob Dole had a great fall.
    —Laurel Whitehead and Whitney Marshall

Reagan's out, Bush's in
Chicago Bulls win again
Desert Storm, Stormin' Norman
Bush's out, global warmin'
Bill and Hillary rule the nation
Whitewater investigation

Oklahoma City bomb
Susan Smith's a bad mom
Valujet, TWA
Branch Davidians, O.J.
Unibomber, gay rights
Bosnia, baseball strikes

Superman paralyzed
Kurt Cobain—suicide

Forrest Gump, Michael Crichton
Hugh Grant, Mike Tyson
Tupac, Easy-E,
Cindy Crawford, Lion King
MTV, Pauly Shore
I can't take it anymore!
        —March McRuiz, Josh Davis, and Mindy Butler

This lesson works extremely well during a poetry unit, but it could be used at any time allusions are first introduced. Students enjoy the process of brainstorming recent well-known people and events, as well as the collaborative writing and presenting. I must say, though, that the use of music doesn't exactly have a taming influence; rather, it tends to enthuse my sophomores.

Kaye Kauffman, Cleburne High School, Cleburne, Texas

Using Scripts to Enhance
Understanding of Literature

As our students read stories and novels, we can't peer into their heads or get computer printouts of their thoughts. How then do we know what students are thinking about what they are reading?

Of the many ways to assess understanding—class discussion, teacher-student conferences, journal writing, tests, essays—one effective method is to let students demonstrate their understanding of a work of literature through script writing. Script writing can be used before, during, and after reading a story, play, autobiography, or novel.

Before reading Guy de Maupassant's "The Necklace," for instance, writing a dialogue between two characters in which they discuss what people think about them, especially about their economic needs and wants, helps students key in on crucial issues of the story, such as Madame Loisel's desire to be stylish even though her economic status makes that difficult. These dialogues reveal that some of the things students desire are also virtually unattainable and thus provide real-life connections to the story's theme.

Script writing effectively reveals what students think during the reading of a text. In *Alicia, My Story,* by Alicia Appleman-Jurman (Bantam Books, 1988), a memoir about survival during World War II, ten-year-old Alicia approaches her rabbi, Reb Srool, hoping he can make sense of what is happening to her family. Troubled himself, he leaves her more confused than ever. At that point in the book, after Alicia's father and her three older brothers have been killed, I want to know what students think about Alicia's plight. My 9th graders find it hard to articulate what they think about these tragic events—class discussions often get hung up on rage at the German S.S. officers who carry out the murderous actions—so one way to get deeper is to ask them to write a dialogue between Alicia and her mother.

The two following samples, read at the beginning or end of a class period, serve as an alternative way to review events that occur in the book and can jump-start discussion by showing what students are thinking and feeling in common.

Sample Dialogue

> Alicia: I'm scared, mama! What's going on?
> Mother: The Germans and Ukrainians don't like us any more. They want us to go away. That is why they tell where we are.
> Alicia: Why do they hate us? We never did anything.
> Mother: Alicia, I don't know why. They are listening to a bad man. And if they don't, they might get killed. He only likes his kind.
> Alicia: Well, what about us? What will we do?
> Mother: All we can do is stick together and pray. We'll make it.
>   —Johnny Devlin and Elaine Strickland

As we near the end of *Alicia, My Story,* I want to know how students are reacting to the brutality described in this memoir, and what they would expect to be done in the aftermath of such a war. One way to do that is to ask students to write a script of a war crime trial, to continue the story. (Additionally, these scripts also show what students know about the trial process, and give them a chance to do a bit of research.)

Excerpt from a Trial Script

> Judge Achner: Boris Mechanger, you are accused of the murder of Frieda Jurman. How do you plead?
> Boris: I plead not guilty.
> Judge: Are you prepared to stand trial for this crime?
> Boris: Yes, sir.
> Judge: The prosecution has the floor.
> Bulio: Hello, Boris, how are you?
> Boris: Well, I have been . . . .
> Bulio: Oh, that's fine and well, sir. Where do you claim to be on the night in question?

Boris: Home in my bed.

Bulio: Do you have anyone who can confirm this?

Boris: Yes, my wife Peppa.

Bulio: Yet Peppa cannot confirm this, correct?

Boris: Yes, that is correct. She is dead.

Bulio: So, technically, no one can confirm that on the night in question you were at home?

Boris: That is technically true.

Bulio: How can you explain the fact that Frieda's daughter had I.D.'d you?

Boris: I cannot, sir.

Bulio: Judge, can we retain Mr. Mechanger for further questioning after our next witness?

Judge: Mr. Mechanger, can you agree to this?

Boris: Yes, sir.

Bulio: I would like to call Alicia Jurman to the stand.

      [Alicia takes the stand]

Judge: Alicia, you have been sworn to tell the truth.

Alicia: That is true.

Bulio: Alicia, you were present during your mother's murder?

Alicia: Yes, that is true.

Bulio: Can you identify the assailant?

Alicia: Yes, I can.

Bulio: Can you please point at him?

             [Alicia points at Boris]

Bulio: Can you please say his name?

Alicia: It was Boris Mechanger—him.

Bulio: You are certain of this?

Alicia: Yes, he pulled out his gun and tried to shoot me. My mother jumped in front of the bullet.

Bulio: And what became of you?

Alicia: I was taken to prison.

Bulio: So you are stating it was Boris Mechanger, and his companion had no part?

Alicia: Yes, the companion never said a word.

Bulio: Thank you Alicia, that is all.

      [Alicia leaves the stand]

  —Annie Petersen and Jaimie Payne

Script writing can be a useful assessment tool and has other benefits. Scripts can be written by pairs or by groups as large as five, providing a vehicle for collaborative writing and encouraging students to talk about characters and issues raised in reading. Writing scripts requires students to imagine or expand on how various characters would talk, and makes students sensitive to the fact that we consciously or unconsciously judge people on how they talk. Lastly, scripts can be rehearsed and performed in the classroom, and offer an accessible and unintimidating way to involve students in public performance.

Students have a lot of fun writing scripts. They frequently beg to have class time to read them all, and their peers hang on every word.

Crag Hill, Moscow High School, Moscow, Idaho

Teaching *Theme* through Children's Books

My seventh-grade students consistently have trouble understanding what *theme* is, often confusing it with plot. In addition, sometimes I'm not sure if students really understand the concept or if they are simply parroting our class discussion. I have found the following exercise helpful both to students' understanding and to my knowledge of how much they understand.

After we have read and discussed theme in various stories, I bring 35 to 40 children's picture books to class and give one to each student. I ask students to read their books and then state or write the theme in one sentence. The brevity and simplicity of the books helps students to pick out the themes, and if any students are still having difficulty, the simple events and messages of the children's books lend themselves to further discussion and illustration of the difference between the storyline or sequence of events (*plot*), and the underlying subject (*theme*).

My students enjoy this activity so much that they often ask to read more than one book. Some books that I've used with success are:

> *The Lorax* by Dr. Seuss
> *Owen* by Kevin Henkes
> *The Table Where Rich People Sit* by Byrd Baylor
> *Stellaluna* by Janell Cannon
> *The Elephant and the Ant* by Bill Peet
> *Hey Al* by Arthur Yorinks

Once the children's books begin to be passed around the room and their themes and plots are discussed and compared, students' understanding is enhanced further by the insights of their peers.

Judith Lewis, North Attleborough Junior High, North Attleborough, Massachusetts

Playing the Role of Dr. Frankenstein

Before class reading of Mary Shelley's *Frankenstein,* I use a prereading exercise that challenges students' imagination and introduces them to some of the issues in the book. I distribute a handout sheet with the following instructions at the top and a blank space below.

Congratulations on your new job with our company! We are glad to have you as our new creative engineer, and, on this your first day, we would like to see your suggestions for a new product. This will be like no other product available because of a discovery recently made by our scientific staff. They have discovered the secret to creating life. Yes, life! After experimenting by creating insects and pigeons, they are ready to move on to more complex tasks. This is where you come in. Our scientists believe they have the capability to create any kind of physical and mental make-up, but they need your advice and imagination. What kind of being should they create? What should it look like? What would it be able to do? What kind of talents would it have? What would be its limitations or weaknesses? How many of these beings would you suggest we create?

Please use the space below to describe your creation in detail and explain your choices. Please provide a visual representation of your creature as well. If you wish, you may label parts that need further description or use arrows to point out special details.

For drawing and/or creating models, I provide crayons, markers, clothes pins, cotton balls, pipe cleaners, and paper clips. Each student plans a creature and describes what it look like, how it acts, what it feels, etc. Many students leave out the *feelings,* which makes the activity even more meaningful once the novel has been read. I hang my students' creations around the room and refer to them during the reading, once students begin to consider the feelings of the monster. This year, as related readings, I also provided articles on cloning and on the education and responsibility of rearing children. These and the experience of playing the role of Dr. Frankenstein added to a new dimension to our reading.

Judith A. Steffen, Oakwood High School, Fithian, Illinois

3   Explorations

Classroom ideas that spark excitement and enthusiasm in your students will maximize learning and growth and help renew both your energy and theirs. The innovative activities in this chapter set the stage for some surprises, as students tackle team teaching, hold silent discussions, revise familiar texts with coined words, and choose community heroes from their own families.

Students as Team Teachers

Did you know that we learn and remember . . .

- 10% of what we hear
- 15% of what we see
- 20% of what we hear and see
- 40% of what we discuss with others
- 80% of what we experience directly or practice
- and 90% of what we attempt to teach to others?

I created this activity after hearing the above statistics at a Johnson and Johnson cooperative learning workshop. This assignment increases student investment and can be effective with a variety of different topics of study.

Guidelines for Students

Have you ever wished you could be the teacher for a day? Well, here's your chance! You will work with one other person to plan, teach, and evaluate a lesson. As a team, you will decide together how to divide the work.

Include the following components in your lesson:

1. Objective: Write this on the board and state it to the class.
2. Motivation: How will you get the class interested in what you have to say?

3. Class Involvement: Will you ask questions of individuals, work in pairs or groups, play a game, ask students to come up and demonstrate, or devise your own strategy?
4. Homework Assignment: The assignment should be something that will take about thirty minutes to complete.
5. Evaluation: How will you assess the students' performance?
6. Visual Aids: Each person must make at least one.

Key Considerations in the Assignment

Presentation
Creativity
Effectiveness
Summary of lesson
Homework assignment
Evaluation
Visuals

The possible range of lessons can be worked out with students. My students have used this technique to teach the components of the research paper, grammar and mechanics, and methods of elaboration. We have videotaped several of the students' lessons to share with younger classes at our school. The students enjoyed this opportunity and watching their creative lessons was inspiring.

Heather Sellers Cocke, South Effingham High School Guyton, Alabama

Silent Discussion

I've struggled with the perennial class-discussion dilemma: the same five or six students participate in every discussion, and getting other students to join in can be nearly impossible. Usually the main problem is that many students are too shy to speak in front of an entire class.

One of my favorite activities is "silent discussion." I often do this after assigning students something to read the previous day. I make a list of twenty or so questions and statements about the reading, preferably controversial ones designed to get students to think and react. I then write each statement or question at the top of a large sheet of paper and tape the sheets on the walls of the classroom.

When the students come to class, I ask them to walk around the room and make comments on the papers. They are to write at least two sentences on each page and then write their initials. They can respond to either the statement at the top of the page or to other students' comments, and may make more than one comment on each page. I encourage the students to draw arrows from their comment to the comment they are responding to. As the students mill around, I check to be sure that the paper discussions are going smoothly. If the students are having a difficult time responding to a particular statement or question or are missing an important point, I sometimes add a comment of my own to that page. When all students have finished writing, I collect the papers and read a few out loud. Then I post all the papers on the class bulletin board.

For example, I used this activity with my ninth graders after they had read *Raymond's Run* by Toni Cade Bambara. To give you an idea of the prompts I use, two statements I posted for this story were: "Squeaky [the main character] would make a great role model for young women," and "If you had to go to the Mayday festival with Squeaky, would you dance around the maypole or run in the race?"

I was amazed at how successful the activity was. Students who were too shy to talk in class wrote long, eloquent comments, and even debated some of the other students' opinions. Then, after I collected all the papers, students enthusiastically asked me to read several of the papers aloud, and congratulated each other for particularly interesting comments. In the following week, many students took a few minutes to read the papers as they hung on the board. This activity is not only applicable for first-year students; I have had similar successes with older students as well.

I was especially impressed that the student comments were sometimes quite astute. I think that students were able to reach a higher level of understanding in this silent discussion than in some oral discussions, for several reasons. First, every student in the classroom made a contribution—not just the more vocal students—so they took the discussion into a new direction. Second, every student had to think about every question, which required concentration and real effort. Third, the students had plenty of time to think of their responses and to express exactly what they meant, which doesn't always happen in the more pressured atmosphere of normal class discussion.

Patricia Brady, Our Lady of Tepeyac High School, Chicago, Illinois

The Learning Journey Portfolio

This is a generic assignment to be used with any extended literature, writing, or general thematic unit. The intent is to make students responsible for evaluating and documenting what they have learned. I give students the following background information and guidelines.

Learning

The goal of every course students take should be learning, where the end product is not a grade, but rather knowledge, understanding, and appreciation for a subject. Learning always involves some kind of change or modification to our knowledge, understanding, or assumptions. It can also mean *deepening* or *broadening* our knowledge base or understanding. Learning can involve *complicating* what we know, and at its most radical modification, changing or *transforming* what we know.

Learning and Evaluation

Learning is not always measured by success or what works. Sometimes, what didn't work or what almost worked may be a better indicator of learning. What is more, learning (at least learning that deepens, complicates, or transforms understanding) is not easily quantified into points and numbers; nor can learning always best be determined by the teacher. Sometimes, you are the best judge of whether learning has occurred. This is why I am asking you to make a learning journey portfolio.

Making a Learning Journey Portfolio

You are to create a portfolio that represents your learning journey during this unit. It will be up to you to think of ways you can best document and explain what you have learned, what you now understand that you didn't understand before, and what ideas you are still churning over in your minds. Consider what "evidence" you might offer that reveals:

A) the extent to which you engaged with discussion, reading, and writing assignments (list or spell these out) we did during this unit,

B) your understanding of the concepts and issues (how many, which ones) we discussed in this unit, and any new avenues of thinking that the concepts and issues might have opened for you,

C) what you know about yourself as a thinker and learner, reader and writer.

Since each of you is unique, I imagine that no two people's portfolios will look the same. Each portfolio should consist of a *selection* of artifacts—writing, assignments, and activities from this unit that best show your learning over the last four weeks.

Each artifact should be accompanied by a reflective commentary (approx. ½ page) that explains what you *think* the artifact shows about what you have learned and now understand about some aspect of the unit. You must include at least five artifacts, but you may include more.

In addition to these smaller reflective commentaries, you will need to write a reflective letter (2–3 pages) that serves as an introduction and overall analysis of the portfolio. What does the portfolio as a whole say about what you have learned?

Think of a title for your portfolio that captures your learning journey so far. In your introductory letter, say why you chose the title you did.

Choose a container for your portfolio that captures your own sense of yourself as a thinker now or the kind of thinker you want to become. Again, explain the significance of the container you chose in your introductory letter.

We will display all the portfolios on the table in front of the room, and then, each of you will have a chance to share some aspect of your portfolio (an artifact, the title, container, etc.) with the rest of the class.

Criteria for Awarding Grades for the Portfolio

- Evidence from categories A, B, and C
- Specificity and depth of analysis in the written reflections
- Completeness and care in construction of the portfolio
- Clarity and thoughtfulness of presentation to the class

Donna Qualley, Western Washington University, Bellingham, Washington

Welcome Back!

Are you tired of having your students interview each other for a first-day-of-school activity? Here are two ideas that I have used with success—they are fun, informative, and less predictable than the traditional ice-breaking interview.

1. As students enter your classroom, allow them to sit anywhere they wish. When class comes to order, ask students to put themselves in alphabetical order, starting with the seats you specify and ending with the opposite end of the room. Set a time limit (I use two minutes) for this task. A pleasant hum of activity arises as students begin questioning each other and repositioning themselves. I've found that since students are talking for a constructive purpose and time is short, the activity never gets out of hand.

2. Here's an activity that allows the class to find out what everyone did over the summer without having to write the "What I Did This Summer" essay. I call this the "Who Did What?" worksheet. Write up approximately ten to fifteen statements that encompass things a student might have done over the summer. A mix of the general and specific is good. In the past, I've included such items as:

a. Saw *Independence Day*
b. Made a new friend
c. Went swimming in a place other than a public pool
d. Went on a trip with a family member

  e. Worked at a fast food restaurant
  f. Read a book that was not required in summer school. (What was it?)

Your students must find someone else in the room (you can include yourself) that has done one of the items on the list. The same person cannot sign any given sheet more than once, although one person may sign for different things from sheet to sheet, depending on what's needed. The first person with a completed sheet wins. (I've given gum or candy as a prize.) Then we take an informal poll around the room, verifying the answers and getting to know each other a little better.

Deborah L. Hansen, Courtland High School, Spotsylvania, Virginia

Let Your Fingers Do the Reading: Using the Yellow Pages as Technical Reading

My students and I have been using the yellow pages of the phone book as a source for real-life technical reading. My classroom observations have shown me that students lack experience reading charts, tables, and other practical, nonfiction material. The yellow pages are something I assumed everybody knew how to use, but as my students put it, "Why should we use the phone book when we can just dial 411?"

In this activity, students use the yellow pages to try to find businesses that offer items or services they might need. In follow-up activities, students may want to brainstorm their own list of items or services; for this initial activity, I provide students with the list below. I've tried to come up with hypothetical situations for which students will not automatically know the name of a business to call.

Through this lesson, I've been able to introduce cross-referencing skills (since, for example, you can't usually find medical help just by looking up "doctors"), refresh alphabetizing skills, and teach specific vocabulary related to students' efforts. Students learn, for example, that "physician" is another word for doctor; that eye doctors are "optometrists"; that lawyers are listed under "attorneys"; and that construction companies are listed under "contractors."

The guidelines I give students are shown below. In the first step, it's a good idea to brainstorm the subject words as a class. Then if no student identifies the key word used in the phone book, you can provide hints or identify it for them so that they will be able to go on to the next step.

Step 1: For each item or service below, name a subject word you could look up in the phone book to try to find that item or service.

1. Plane tickets
2. Halloween costumes
3. A doctor for your dog
4. A doctor for your three-year-old cousin
5. A ride to the bus station
6. Someone to fix your kitchen sink
7. A place where you can buy a used stereo
8. A place to buy flowers for your mom
9. A DJ for your next party
10. Someone to come clean your carpets
11. A place that will help you find a job
12. An apartment complex near where you now live

Step 2: The items and services we've discussed are listed in the chart below. Look up two businesses that can provide each item or service, preferably businesses that are close to where you live. In the spaces provided, write the subject word or phrase that you used to find the businesses, the names of the two businesses, and their phone numbers.

Service or item needed	Subject	Business name and phone number
1. Plane tickets	_____	_____
2. Halloween costumes	_____	_____
3. A doctor for your dog	_____	_____
4. A doctor for your three-year old cousin	_____	_____
5. A ride to the bus station	_____	_____
6. Someone to fix your kitchen sink	_____	_____
7. A place where you can buy a used stereo	_____	_____
8. A place to buy flowers for your mom	_____	_____
9. A DJ for your next party	_____	_____
10. Someone to come clean your carpets	_____	_____
11. A place that will help you find a job	_____	_____
12. An apartment complex near where you now live	_____	_____

My students have enjoyed the brainstorming and research involved in this activity, and they relish learning skills that they can use right away. We are now expanding our phone book exploration to the information pages at the beginning (or, in some areas, the center) of the phone book, which include a city map, street index, a map of telephone area codes and time zones, and a list of government offices.

Jennifer Gude, Maitland Middle School, Maitland, Florida

Connecting Conflict Resolution to Current Events

As my school system began using programs to teach conflict resolution and mediation strategies several years ago, I felt that my urban middle school students needed to have additional grounding in these vital life skills.

We first talked as a class about the concepts of "conflict resolution," "conflict management," "compromise," and "third-party mediation," including brainstorming our own definitions of these terms. Students also brainstormed situations that might benefit from conflict resolution methods, and we touched on the subject of civil suits and court cases. We also discussed the pros and cons of taking a problem "to a higher authority" such as the court system, versus trying to resolve it on one's own. Points that students felt were important included the following:

- Conflict resolution requires active participation by those directly involved.
- In conflict resolution, both parties cooperate together as equals to come to an agreement.
- A court case usually leaves one party a loser.
- Conflict resolution is more informal than a court decision, which can involve punishment.

I asked students if they felt that the attention and time spent on teaching conflict management was justified. In general, my students felt that it was. One student noted that many of his friends had personal conflicts in their lives that the process of conflict resolution could help them deal with on their own. Other students described how the conflict resolution principles could be applied to ongoing disputes in their apartment buildings and in particular school settings, even in situations with teachers.

Next, I explained to students that we were going to identify conflicts in the news that we thought could benefit from conflict resolution or mediation. I distributed newspapers to teams of two and three students each. Students went to work in their groups with much clipping and quiet conversation. As I circulated through the classroom, I was pleased to see that no team was having trouble finding disputes covered in the news.

When the teams shared their disputes the next day, the range was quite impressive: Among the conflicts selected in a single news day were:

- The John Gotti appeal effort
- The dispute that led to the ejection of Patrick Ewing and Derrick Coleman from a basketball game
- The windshield dispute between Jack Nicholson and Robert Blank
- The internalized conflict a drunken driver felt as he dealt with the fact that he ran over three family members
- Various conflicts in South Africa as individuals and pro-apartheid and anti-apartheid groups prepared for the open democratic elections

The next period was devoted to individual writing based on the news stories. Students could choose from a variety of possible formats, such as the following: an essay detailing a newspaper conflict and the disputants' positions; an editorial column in the voice of one disputant, advocating his or her position; an essay offering a mediated resolution of the conflict; a script for a short scene between the disputants, in which they attempt to resolve their conflict; a critique of the situation, as described in the newspaper article, in terms of conflict resolution principles and how they were or were not used. In addition to these formats, some students used the format of a storyboard panel to depict interactions between the disputants and to illustrate the conflict resolution process.

These activities helped show students the value of the conflict resolution process, and the link to current news stories highlighted the ways in which conflict resolution can proactively influence civic, social, and global events.

Rose Reissman, Community School District # 1, Brooklyn, New York

Wockyjabber

Keep this lesson light. *Wockyjabber* is not a grammar lesson, nor should it be turned into one. Rather, it is a form of wordplay (i.e., playing around with words), an essential human use of language consistent with the work of James Moffett and Betty Jane Wagner as well as Linda Gibson Geller. (See Moffett and Wagner's *Student Centered Language Arts and Reading K–12,* 4th edition [Heinemann, 1993] and Geller's *Wordplay and Language Learning for Children* [NCTE, 1985].) Having said that, students do, in fact, reinforce grammar concepts in the activity (either conscious knowledge of grammar or their subconscious understanding dictated by syntax). That should suffice.

Step 1 (10–15 minutes): Read Lewis Carroll's nonsense poem "Jabberwocky" aloud—skillfully with whatever bombast you can muster! Pretend like it means something. Allow students to respond. Nudge them with questions like "What's this about, would you say?" or "How do you feel about what happened to . . . ?"

Once the secret's out, give students copies of the poem. Then on the board list several nouns, verbs, and adjectives that Lewis Carroll coined in the poem. If students don't know parts of speech, you can list *things, actions,* and *attributes/describers.*

Step 2 (15 minutes): Distribute to pairs and threesomes examples of discourse such as: a Dear Abby letter, a letter to the editor, a menu from a local eatery, a brochure advertising a local attraction, the Gettysburg Address, morning announcements, lyrics to a hit song, Lady Macbeth's "Out Out" soliloquy, and so on. Have students rewrite their text, substituting as they do at least three verbs, nouns, and adjectives they coin. (For less sophisticated kids, highlight selected words to replace using three different marker colors, yellow for verbs, pink for nouns, and so forth.)

Step 3 (10+ minutes): Read aloud, giggle, enjoy!

Jim Brewbaker, Columbus State University, Columbus, Georgia

Indexes

Author Index

Subject Index

Classroom Management

Discussion

Interdisciplinary

Language Exploration

Literature